This journal is intended to stimulate the imagination while you write. Don't worry about mistakes, this is your journal and no one has to read it but you!

Tips:
Show, don't tell. This means that you should describe the setting and actions to help the reader experience the story.

Try describing the scene by involving the senses. What does the air smell like? How does the fog feel against the skin? How do the raindrops taste?

There are 60 prompts for 60 days of practice. And remember, the more you write, the more your writing improves.

Think hard about your very first memory. What is it? How old were you? Write about it here.

Write a scene that starts with "If all my wishes came true, I would..."

You live in a house with only one window. What do you see through it each day?

You find a time machine and step inside. You close the door and dial a year in the past. What year did you dial and why?

_____

_____

_____

_____

_____

_____

_____

_____

_____

_____

_____

_____

_____

_____

_____

_____

_____

_____

You step back into the time machine and choose another year. This time further back in time. You open the door and there you are. What do you see? Who do you meet?

Write about it here.

_____

_____

_____

_____

_____

_____

_____

_____

_____

_____

_____

_____

_____

_____

_____

_____

_____

_____

_____

What are some of your favorite names? Why? Write about it here.

What do you struggle with the most? Write about it.

Jane Howard said, "Call it a clan, call it a network, call it a tribe, call it a family. Whatever you call it, whoever you are, you need one."

What does this quote mean to you? Write it here.

_____

_____

_____

_____

_____

_____

_____

_____

_____

_____

_____

_____

_____

_____

_____

_____

_____

_____

Imagine that we had no computers, cell phones, or TVs. Write about how you would spend your days.

List 5 places you have visited that you love and write why you love them.

Write about your favorite book.

Write a story that begins with "The wind lifted me so high it...."

_____

_____

_____

_____

_____

_____

_____

_____

_____

_____

_____

_____

_____

_____

_____

_____

_____

_____

_____

Create a brand new country with its own language, traditions, foods, and holidays.

Write a story titled "The Llama Who Never Slept."

Finish this thought, "If I could come dressed as a character from a book it would be_____because..."

_____

_____

_____

_____

_____

_____

_____

_____

_____

_____

_____

_____

_____

_____

_____

_____

_____

_____

_____

_____

My happy place is _____, because...

In 100 years in the future, what will people say about life in our time right now?

Write a scene or a poem that includes these three things: a pink flower, a cake, and a guitar.

_____

_____

_____

_____

_____

_____

_____

_____

_____

_____

_____

_____

_____

_____

_____

_____

_____

_____

_____

What do you think the world needs now?

What do you consider your greatest accomplishment?

What do you think about people polluting the environment?

_____

_____

_____

_____

_____

_____

_____

_____

_____

_____

_____

_____

_____

_____

_____

_____

_____

_____

Write a short narrative (fiction or nonfiction) where this is your first sentence, "I was so mortified, I wanted to crawl in a hole!"

List some of the traditions in your family. Pick one and write about it.

My hero is...

You are walking down a paved road and you come across one glove leaning against a curb. Write a story about how the glove got there.

Write about the difference between dreams and goals.

You are moving to the moon and you can only take 15 items with you. What would they be and why?

Write a story about a boy that woke up and was 6 inches tall.

Write a self-portrait.

Write a scene that happens between a man in a wheelchair and a teenager.

Pick two characters from different books you've read this year and have them get in an argument about something (e.g., who has suffered more, who has had a happier life, etc.).

Write a scene that starts with "I wish I could learn _____ because..."

Tell this story: "There it was, finally. Our island. Our very own island. It looked beautiful above the waves of fog, but there was still one question to be answered: why had they sold it to us for only five dollars?"

_____

_____

_____

_____

_____

_____

_____

_____

_____

_____

_____

_____

_____

_____

_____

_____

_____

_____

The thing I wish people understood about me is_____

Write five complete sentences that begin with the words "I am happiest when..."

Write a story that begins with "I thought it was going to be a regular Christmas and then…"

Find a picture or image from a magazine. Attach it and write about it here.

_____

_____

_____

_____

_____

_____

_____

_____

_____

_____

_____

_____

_____

_____

_____

_____

_____

_____

Write a poem titled "Summer Breeze."

Write five complete sentences that begin with the words "I will never forget…"

Write about your favorite memory of family spending time together.

Woodrow Wilson said, "Friendship is the only cement that will hold the world together."

Use this quote as a prompt for free writing.

Maya Angelou said, "I've learned that you can tell a lot about a person by the way s/he handles these three things: a rainy day, lost luggage, and tangled Christmas tree lights." Tell a story in which a character has to deal with one or all of these scenarios. How does the character respond?

_____

_____

_____

_____

_____

_____

_____

_____

_____

_____

_____

_____

_____

_____

_____

_____

_____

Imagine in the future when we can travel to Mars for vacations.

What will that vacation look like? How will you get there? What will be on Mars when you arrive?

_____

_____

_____

_____

_____

_____

_____

_____

_____

_____

_____

_____

_____

_____

_____

_____

Create a new dessert and give it a name.What are the ingredients? How do you eat it?

If you could go back in time and meet a person that is no longer with us, who would it be?

What would you ask them?

_____

_____

_____

_____

_____

_____

_____

_____

_____

_____

_____

_____

_____

_____

_____

_____

_____

_____

_____

If dogs could speak, what would they say about humans?

Write a scene where a person is doing something funny while two dogs observe. What would the dogs say to each other?

Write a story about a girl that went to sleep and woke up 10 feet tall.

My favorite book this year has been_____. Write about the reason it is your favorite book here.

_____

_____

_____

_____

_____

_____

_____

_____

_____

_____

_____

_____

_____

_____

_____

_____

_____

_____

Pick a member of your family and write about them. Why are they special?

_____

_____

_____

_____

_____

_____

_____

_____

_____

_____

_____

_____

_____

_____

_____

_____

_____

If you could be any animal living or extinct, which would it be? Explain with writing.

I was proud when I...

I am afraid to _____, because...

My family is...

Think of two animals. Write them on the first line.

Now write a short story where both of them appear.

Write a short scene that starts with the line "When I walked outside this morning, the air smelled like..."

Find 10 inspirational quotes. Write them here.

If you could travel anywhere in the world and leave tomorrow, where would you go?

What is your favorite holiday? What makes this holiday special?

What is your favorite day of the week? Why?

William Shakespeare wrote that "Conversation should be pleasant without scurrility, witty without affectation, free without indecency, learned without conceitedness, novel without falsehood."

Write about what this quote means to you.

Thank you for purchasing our book. If you enjoyed the contents we would appreciate a sincere review.

We accept custom orders.

If you would like to contact us directly, you can email us at customerservice@bykateandsophie.com

Or visit us at ByKateandSophie.com

Made in the USA
Middletown, DE
25 May 2022

66226226R00068